WEIGHT WATCHERS®

101 SECRETS FOR SUCCESS

*Weight-Loss Tips from Weight Watchers Leaders,
Staff and Members*

MACMILLAN ◆ USA

MACMILLAN GENERAL REFERENCE
A Simon & Schuster Macmillan Company
1633 Broadway
New York, NY 10019-6785

Library of Congress Cataloging-in-Publication Data
Weight Watchers 101 secrets for success : weight loss tips from Weight Watchers leaders.
        p.   cm.
Includes index.
ISBN: 0-02-860986-7 (alk. paper)
1. Weight loss.   2. Weight loss—Psychological aspects.   3. Weight Watchers
International.   I. Weight Watchers International.
                RM222.2.W2987 1996
        613.2'5—dc20   95-35425
                CIP

Book design by Anne Scatto/Pixel Press
Manufactured in the United States of America
10 9 8 7 6 5 4

Introduction

Weight Watchers meetings are unique because leaders and staff members have all been through the Weight Watchers program, and have achieved and continue to maintain their weight goals.

We dedicate this book to those motivated women and men who inspire a million members around the world each week with their personal stories, support, advice, encouragement and humor. They are committed to helping everyone who walks through the door to reach their personal goals.

Over the more than 30 years since Weight Watchers was founded, the wisdom and experience of these leaders and their staffs have helped members stay focused on their objectives, overcome obstacles and enjoy the process.

Here, for the first time, is a collection of uplifting and practical weight-loss tips to help and inspire you, too.

*H*op, skip and shuffle your pounds away by tap dancing to the oldies.

Can you wiggle your foot? That's all it takes to get started.

Squeeze into a pair of tights, find a class and don't worry

about your age because these days even grandmothers are tapping.

L. S.
North York, Ontario, Canada

I always keep a "skinny" skirt or pants handy, which I try on
often to see how far my weight loss has progressed.
This way, even if the scales don't show the pounds, I can still see
I've lost inches. It really makes me feel better, and I'm more
determined than ever to stay on my weight-loss program.

S. L. W.
Spring Hill, Florida

*I*nternal motivation—"I'm doing this for me"—is a powerful tool, far stronger than trying to lose weight for others or some special event. And once you have incorporated and learned to live with the basics, they're yours for life.

M. G.
Atlantis, Florida

I fool myself into thinking I have potato chips on my lunch plate by slicing an apple or pear into rounds. Sounds simple and silly, but each crunchy bite satisfies my craving.

V. H.
Bedford, Texas

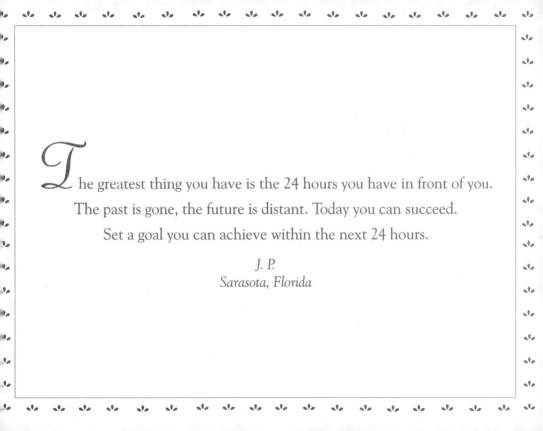

The greatest thing you have is the 24 hours you have in front of you.
The past is gone, the future is distant. Today you can succeed.
Set a goal you can achieve within the next 24 hours.

J. P.
Sarasota, Florida

*W*hen on a weight-loss program, instead of focusing on the total amount of weight you want to lose, concentrate on following the food plan one day at a time. Put a magnetic board on your refrigerator, and for each pound lost add a letter until you have spelled out s-u-c-c-e-s-s-f-u-l. This is a positive reminder that you've already lost ten pounds!

R. K.
Brooklyn, New York

$\mathcal{M}$otivation is what gets you started.

Good habits are what keep you going.

C. B.
Fort Lee, New Jersey

*P*ortion out "trigger" foods at a time when you're in control, like first thing in the morning. Place foods in sealable bags or containers and enjoy the right-size helpings later in the day.

M. J. J.
Ogdensburg, Wisconsin

$\mathcal{R}$emember—losing "only" one pound
a week adds up to 52 pounds a year!

M. W.
Timonium, Maryland

$\mathcal{W}$riting down my feelings and thoughts in a journal during my weight loss has helped me. I get the words on paper and later on I can go back to read and reflect. Something I heard at a meeting really inspired me: "Once we know what we value, it is easier to go about living with a focus and a direction."

B. A. C.
Shoreview, Minnesota

*E*xercise can enhance your weight loss as well as
make you look and feel great.

E. K.
Brentwood, Tennessee

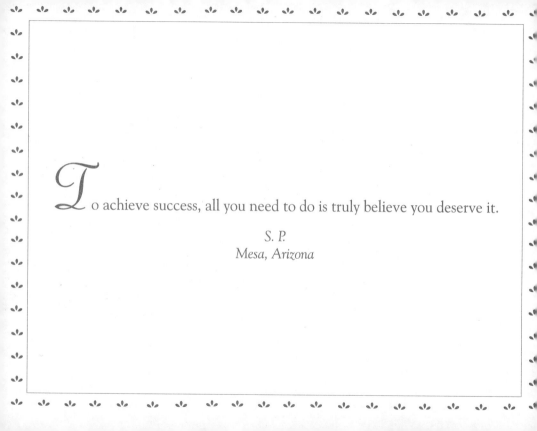

*T*o achieve success, all you need to do is truly believe you deserve it.

S. P.
Mesa, Arizona

W hen eating out, plan what to order in advance and ask for a Styrofoam carton with your food. Put the "extras" in the carton first to avoid eating too much.

M. J. J.
Ogdensburg, Wisconsin

$\mathcal{R}$efuse to accept missteps as failures.
Try to identify the cause and learn from the experience.

V. E. D.
Hicksville, New York

*W*hen I started my weight-loss plan, I wrote myself a letter
and said good-bye to the fat. I listed every reason to hate
the extra weight and why it kept me from doing what I wanted.
I mailed the letter to myself and read it every time I wanted to overeat.

S. W.
Spring Hill, Florida

*N*ever get too tired, too hungry, too lonely.

C. T.
Chicago, Illinois

*A*lways try something new: food, exercise or a recipe.
If you love it, make a deposit into your lifestyle bank.
The wealthier it is, the easier it is to maintain.
Remember, you can withdraw only if you make deposits.

S. B.
Mahopac, New York

*S*uccess is a journey, not a destination. Weight loss is a process. Just being part of the process means you are succeeding.

V. H.
North Platte, Nebraska

*I*t's the small things you change that make the biggest difference.

Drink a little more water. Take a few more steps.

Eat a few more veggies. Get a little closer to your goal!

D. S.
Coopersburg, Pennsylvania

*E*xercising is one of the most important things you can do
to help your weight-loss plan. It speeds weight loss,
makes you look and feel better and reduces stress.

M. S.
Wilkes Barre, Pennsylvania

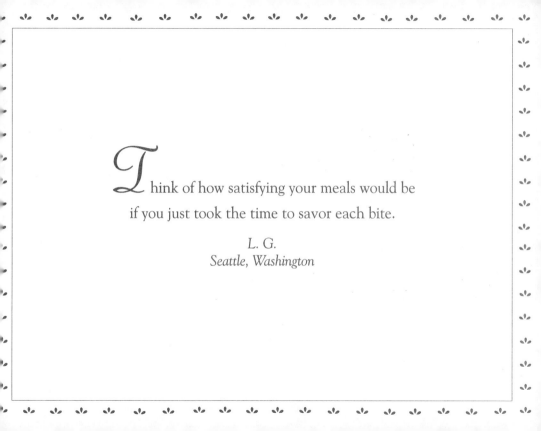

*T*hink of how satisfying your meals would be
if you just took the time to savor each bite.

L. G.
Seattle, Washington

$\mathcal{D}$on't think of "losing" weight. Think of "removing" it. You "lose" something carelessly. You "remove" something deliberately, with great care, because it is no longer desirable and you wish to be free of it permanently. Choose your words with care—they affect your attitude and belief system.

D. M. B.
Seattle, Washington

*W*hat you did is not important. What you learned from it is.

T. M.
Wales, Massachusetts

*D*o you remember the "last straw"—the thing that made you
decide to lose weight once and for all? I won't forget.
I keep a piece of straw by my mirror. It reminds me of how I felt
right before I made the commitment to reach my goal.

C. W.
Tahuya, Washington

*A*pproach vacations, holidays and special occasions realistically.
Perhaps during these times you should focus on
maintaining the weight loss you have already achieved.

C. E.
Phoenix, Arizona

$\mathcal{T}$ake body measurements weekly. My weight at the scale plateaued for ten weeks, but my body measurements kept getting smaller. Oh, what a wonderful feeling—seeing that difference!

K. F.
Opelousas, Louisiana

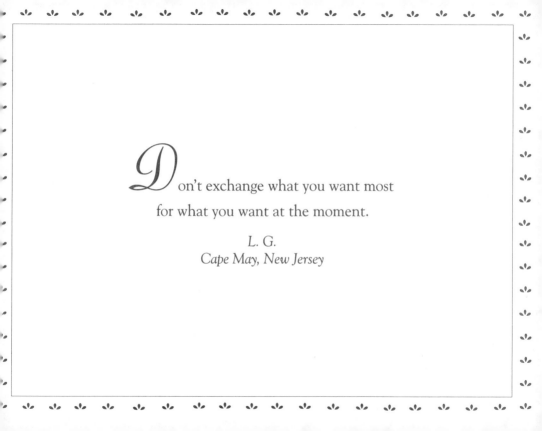

*D*on't exchange what you want most
for what you want at the moment.

L. G.
Cape May, New Jersey

$\mathcal{T}$emptation to give in to:

If you feel you deserve a treat, give in to the urge to treat

yourself to a hairdo, new make-up, a bunch of flowers!

A. F.
New York, New York

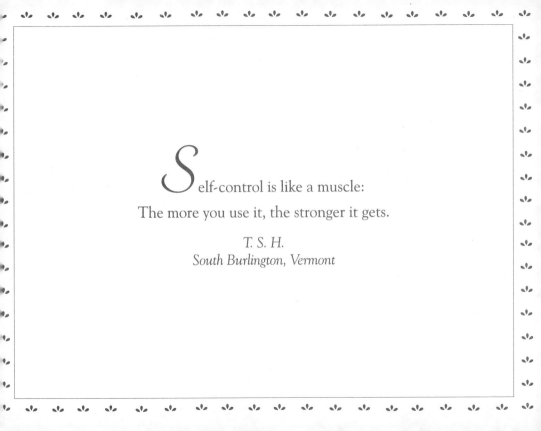

$\mathcal{S}$elf-control is like a muscle:
The more you use it, the stronger it gets.

T. S. H.
South Burlington, Vermont

*W*hen my dessert alarm won't quit clanging, I fix a serving of
oatmeal in the microwave, stir in some spreadable fruit
and get a treat that my body approves of.

P. S.
Vancouver, Washington

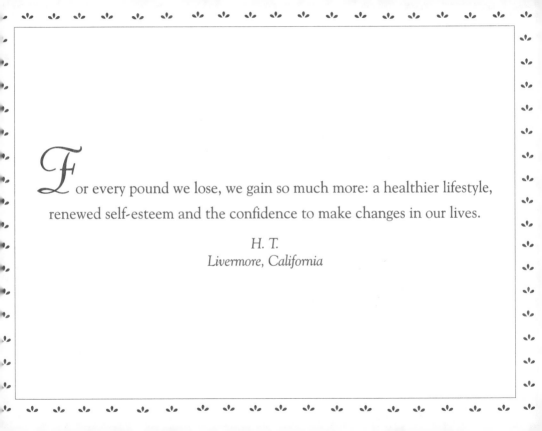

*F*or every pound we lose, we gain so much more: a healthier lifestyle, renewed self-esteem and the confidence to make changes in our lives.

H. T.
Livermore, California

*A*s a busy mother of three children, I often find it impossible to exercise. My solution? Play with the kids! Children get most of their exercise through playing, and so can we!

S. R. L.
Commack, New York

*Y*ou can't eat what you don't buy. Plan. Make a list.
Buy only what is written. Never shop hungry!

M. W.
Swanton, Maryland

$\mathcal{N}$ow, right at this moment, you are perfectly all right, just the way you are. You need to accept this.

M. T.
Brookfield, Connecticut

$\mathcal{W}$hen you want to give up, ask yourself, "What is the alternative?"
When you realize that it's gaining more and more weight
and feeling worse and worse, you'll get back on track!

J. C.
Whitestone, New York

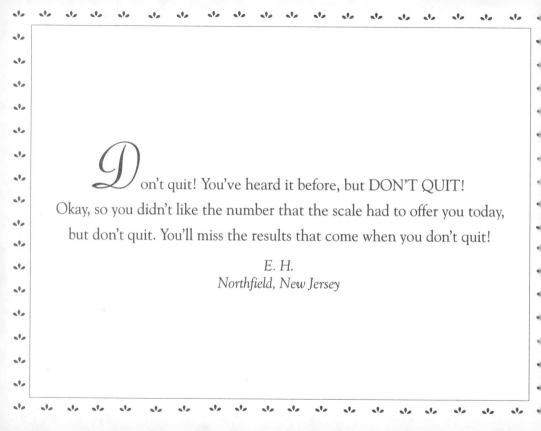

$\mathcal{D}$on't quit! You've heard it before, but DON'T QUIT!
Okay, so you didn't like the number that the scale had to offer you today,
but don't quit. You'll miss the results that come when you don't quit!

E. H.
Northfield, New Jersey

$\mathcal{I}$ keep track of all the food I've resisted each week. It's soon clear as to how many calories I used to eat. Then I give myself credit for being in control and how strong my willpower is when I want to cheat.

S. L. W.
Spring Hill, Florida

*I*f you are angry or upset or under stress, ask yourself—
do I need something to eat or is something eating me?

W. J. O.
Brooklyn, New York

*A*ny exercise is better than none.

R. P.
Rigby, Idaho

$\mathcal{M}$aking just one small change each day can bring you closer to your dream. Start with something as simple as walking around the block or politely declining a second helping.

H. T.
Livermore, California

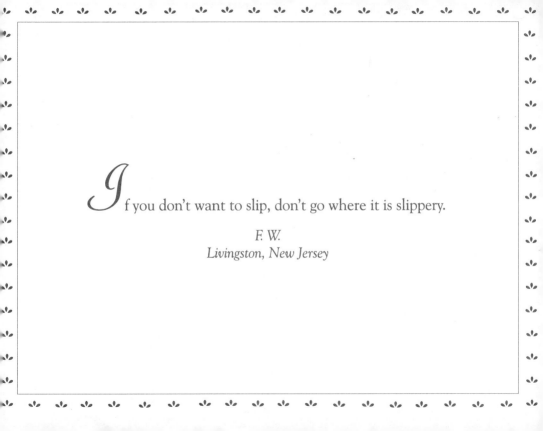

$\mathcal{I}$f you don't want to slip, don't go where it is slippery.

F. W.
Livingston, New Jersey

*W*hen my members become discouraged by a small weight loss, I tell them to reverse it. How would they feel if they *gained* one pound each week? This usually turns their thinking around!

L. K.
Aberdeen, New Jersey

$\mathcal{T}$ake charge while shopping! Never go to the supermarket hungry. People who shop on a full stomach tend to buy more nutritious fruits and vegetables and less high-fat junk food.

L. T.
High Bridge, New Jersey

*L*osing weight in a healthy way takes time and patience.
Allow yourself to experience both and enjoy the rewards.

R. R.
Bound Brook, New Jersey

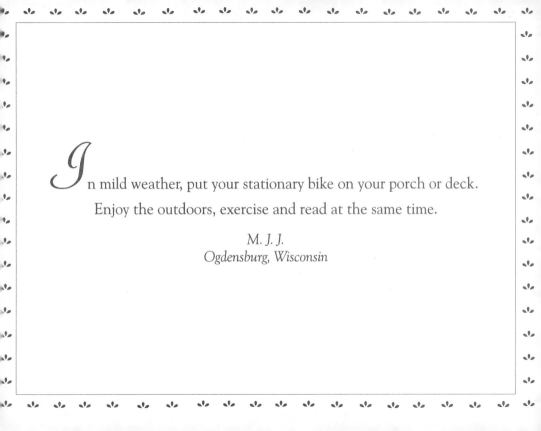

*I*n mild weather, put your stationary bike on your porch or deck. Enjoy the outdoors, exercise and read at the same time.

M. J. J.
Ogdensburg, Wisconsin

Social events do not have to be minefields. Visualize yourself

at the party, meeting new people and having a good time.

Plan what you will eat and stop when you've eaten it.

M. B.
Cornwall, New York

$\mathcal{T}$ime is going to pass whether you lose weight or not.
Isn't it wonderful if, as it passes, the pointer on the scale
is going in the right direction?

M. R.
Los Angeles, California

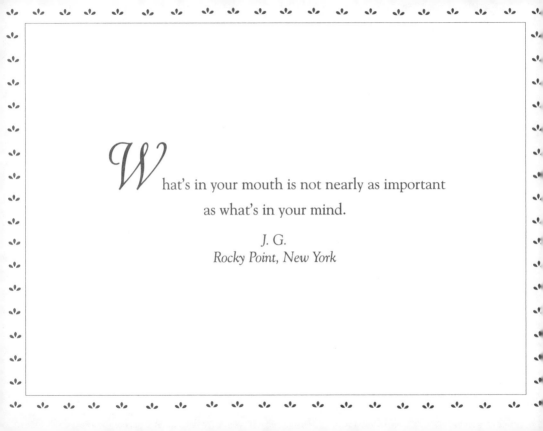

_W_hat's in your mouth is not nearly as important

as what's in your mind.

J. G.
Rocky Point, New York

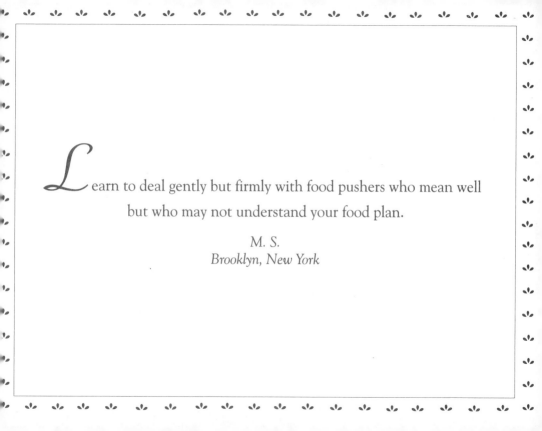

$\mathcal{L}$ earn to deal gently but firmly with food pushers who mean well
but who may not understand your food plan.

M. S.
Brooklyn, New York

$\mathcal{T}$ry at least one new recipe each week—it can keep you from getting bored and help you stay on track.

L. S.
Santa Maria, California

$\mathcal{N}$ever underestimate the power of group support.

C. M.
Waterman, Illinois

*W*hen you get ready to eat, take a minute while drinking
a glass of water to decide, "By eating this, am I getting
closer to or farther from my goal?"
This will help you to make a food decision.

C. S.
Manchester, Maryland

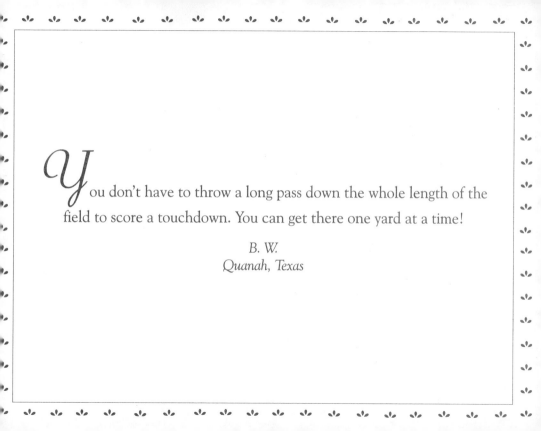

$\mathcal{Y}$ou don't have to throw a long pass down the whole length of the field to score a touchdown. You can get there one yard at a time!

B. W.
Quanah, Texas

$\mathcal{M}$ake a commitment to exercise.

Schedule regular activity into your day.

J. C.
New York, New York

$\mathcal{A}$sk yourself if you are truly hungry before you open the

pantry or fridge for a snack. If the answer is yes,

wait ten minutes and ask yourself the question again.

G. M. G.
Kingston, New York

*D*on't be discouraged if you don't lose weight quickly.
If you lose too fast, you're probably not learning
how to eat properly or how to change your habits.

R. V.
Arlington, Virginia

$\mathcal{I}$ plan my meals in advance, usually by the week;
therefore, I give a great deal of thought to the actual planning.
I shop from a grocery list, I buy very little "snacking food"
and I always reach for low-fat, sugarless items.

M. W.
Swanton, Maryland

$\mathcal{T}$ry visualizing each quarter-pound weight loss as a stick of butter melting away. That's a great way to feel positive about a small loss at weigh-in.

B. S. L.
New York, New York

*I*t's easier to act your way into a new way of thinking than to think your way into a new way of acting. Don't just think about it—do it! Take the plunge and move toward your goal.

A. H.
Cheshire, Connecticut

*T*hink you're hungry? Take the "Green Bean Test." Ask yourself, "Would eating green beans suffice?" If the answer is yes, you're probably really hungry and should eat, but within your program guidelines.

D. L.
San Diego, California

$\mathcal{R}$elax your body, not your efforts.

A. F.
New York, New York

A large steaming mug of decaf coffee or tea with sugar substitute and skim milk fills my stomach, soothes my nerves and can be purchased on the road.

K. P.
San Jose, California

$\mathcal{I}$t's not selfish to put yourself and your needs first. When you improve the quality of your life, everyone around you will reap the benefits.

G. M. G.
Kingston, New York

*W*hen a craving strikes, I identify it, match it with a fat-free recipe and plan it in. Then it becomes real and does not destroy my food plan.

B. M.
Apple Valley, Minnesota

$\mathcal{T}$ ake time for yourself, be good to yourself and make your own dreams come true. Learn the value of your own importance— recognize what you are worth. Accept the challenge—realize that a slip is not the end of your goals and dreams.

Go with your dreams!

C. R.
Barrington, New Jersey

$\mathcal{T}$o coat your whole salad with the correct
portion of dressing, first measure out your dressing and pour
into a resealable plastic bowl. Then add the salad ingredients,
put the lid on securely and shake like crazy!
Your salad will be nicely coated with just the right amount of dressing.

J. A.
Lake Villa, Illinois

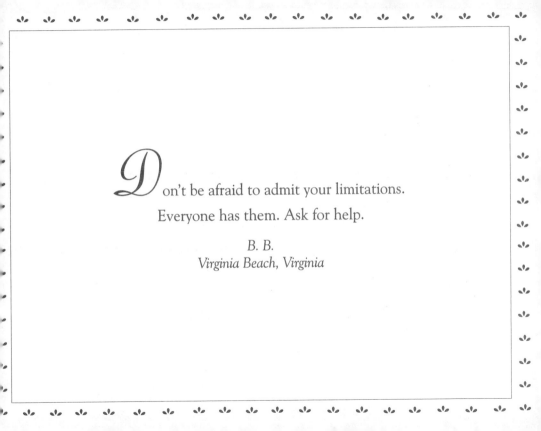

*D*on't be afraid to admit your limitations.
Everyone has them. Ask for help.

B. B.
Virginia Beach, Virginia

*W*hen you are faced with a food buffet, fill a plate with salad while checking out the rest of the food.
Eat and enjoy your salad, then go back a second time for the entrée you have selected. You'll be less hungry and more in control.

B. F. S.
Bristol, Connecticut

$\mathcal{M}$easure success in more than pounds. Take pride in feeling better and healthier, looking better, wearing a smaller size, managing stress without turning to food.

M. M.
New York, New York

*T*ake responsibility for yourself. No one can make you eat;
only you can make that choice.

T. S. H.
South Burlington, Vermont

$\mathcal{B}$e kind to yourself. Look for improvement, not perfection.

F. B.
Comanche, Iowa

*S*ince I already know what the food I'm craving tastes like, I imagine myself chewing it, swallowing it and it's gone!

L. G.
Kings Park, New York

$\mathcal{E}$xercise is crucial to long-term weight control,
so find a way to make it permanent. I had problems
until I began listening to books on tape while working out.
This works for me; find what works for you!

D. T.
Dwight, Illinois

*A*dmit to yourself and realize that you didn't put it on in one day, and therefore you're not going to take it off in one day, either!

M. G.
Asheville, North Carolina

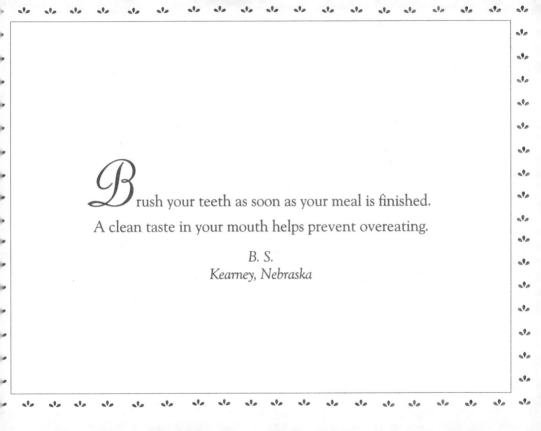

*B*rush your teeth as soon as your meal is finished.
A clean taste in your mouth helps prevent overeating.

B. S.
Kearney, Nebraska

$\mathcal{Y}$ou can't always change your lifestyle to fit the program. Instead, find ways to make the program fit your lifestyle.

B. J. M.
Davenport, Iowa

he greatest weight loss is usually achieved in the first few weeks.
Don't blame yourself if it then slows down, but keep up your
motivation and step up your activity.

L. T.
High Bridge, New Jersey

I always keep sugar-free ice pops in the freezer. If I want to stick something in my mouth, these have only eight calories and have to be eaten slowly, so I have time to think about what's going on.

D. A.
Abilene, Texas

*W*hen following my food plan, I say, "I am thin" 20 times each day.

This helps my mind quickly realize the fact that

I really am thin, and when I do get to my weight goal

it will make me feel good about myself, too.

S. L. W.
Spring Hill, Florida

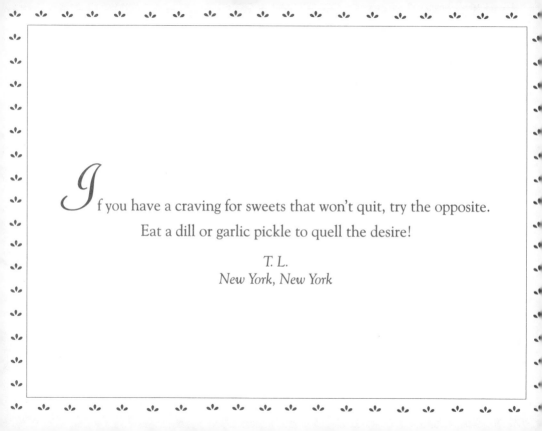

$\mathcal{I}$f you have a craving for sweets that won't quit, try the opposite. Eat a dill or garlic pickle to quell the desire!

T. L.
New York, New York

*D*on't feed a mood food.

E. R. C.
Agawam, Massachusetts

$\mathcal{T}$aking control of my life, that's success!
I am the only person who has control over what I eat.
I am the only one putting food in my mouth;
therefore, I am in control of my weight loss.
I like being in control.

N. B.
Naperville, Illinois

*L*isten to your binges. They are signals you send to yourself.
Perhaps you have allowed your life to get out of balance.
Pay attention to those signals and take remedial action—
it's a key maintenance skill.

D. F.
Nashville, Tennessee

$\mathcal{B}$e patient. Benefits won't show overnight.

But they *will* come.

M. E.
Parker, Colorado

$\mathcal{B}$e true to yourself. When you cheat constantly, you're not hurting

anyone but yourself. You're not hurting your friends,

your family, just *yourself.*

M. G.
Asheville, North Carolina

To avoid the "Monster Cravings" in my life, I've stopped eating sugar.
That seems to be the key to closing the door to Cravings.
On rare occasions when I let him in, I take him back out by
going for a walk. That gives me time to tell him, "I'm in control."
I'm down 34 pounds, and he rarely visits anymore.

L. C.
Calgary, Alberta, Canada

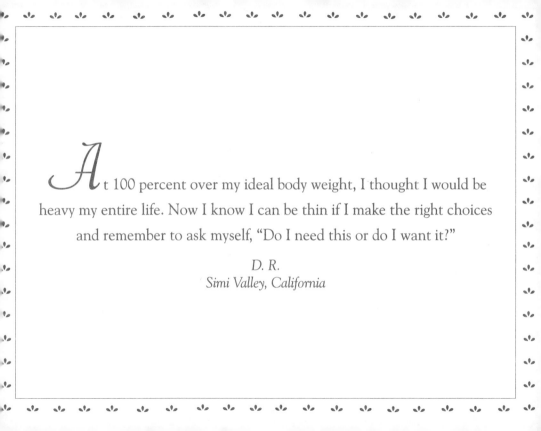

$\mathcal{A}$t 100 percent over my ideal body weight, I thought I would be heavy my entire life. Now I know I can be thin if I make the right choices and remember to ask myself, "Do I need this or do I want it?"

D. R.
Simi Valley, California

$\mathcal{T}$hink substitution, not deprivation.
Deprivation is not a long-term solution.

A. W.
San Clemente, California

$\mathcal{E}$at consciously. Slow down. Be aware of what you are putting in your mouth and how it is nourishing your body.

C. R.
Kansas City, Kansas

$\mathcal{N}$ ever forget why you wanted to lose weight. When you are bored or
"tired of doing this," take out some old "before" photos
to remember how you felt and why you wanted to change.
Never be too hard on yourself; and don't forget that losing weight
means changing behavior, which takes time and patience.

C. M.
Fremont, California

R...ecognize

E...very

W...eight-loss

A...ccomplishment

R...ewards

D...evelop

S...uccess

D. L.
Freehold, New Jersey

$\mathcal{N}$othing tastes as good as thin feels.

D. B.
Clarksville, Indiana

$\mathcal{R}$edefine normal. Normal is lots of veggies, less fat, moderate exercise, adequate water and a positive attitude.

J. M.
Reno, Nevada

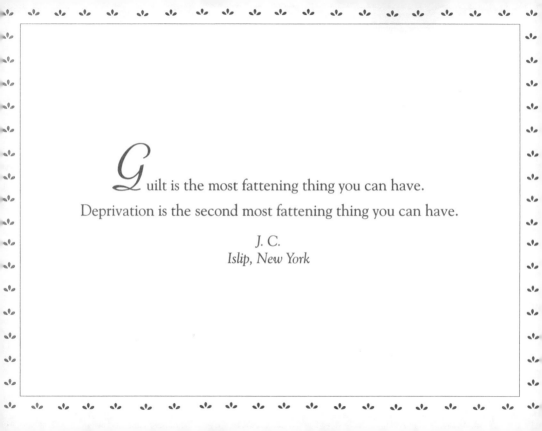

$\mathcal{G}$uilt is the most fattening thing you can have.

Deprivation is the second most fattening thing you can have.

J. C.
Islip, New York

$\mathcal{L}$ ive as if you'll always be at your ideal weight—
even while you're losing it. This means being more active.
Find ways to move more and make activity a part of your life.

T. A. F.
Port Angeles, Washington

$\mathcal{W}$hat happened is in the past; and while I can't change yesterday,

I can change tomorrow.

B. B.
West Liberty, Iowa

*I*f your eating is out of control at 10:00 A.M., you can be
back in control at 10:01 A.M. Being out of control
can last for only a moment, if you let it.

D. R.
Portsmouth, Virginia

$\mathcal{T}$aking off weight is one of the most challenging and creative endeavors you can undertake. Think of your decision as a gift you are giving yourself, not as a deprivation period in your life. You will thank yourself for this gift more and more as time goes on and the weight comes off. And, of course, you are worth it!

G. G.
Baltimore, Maryland

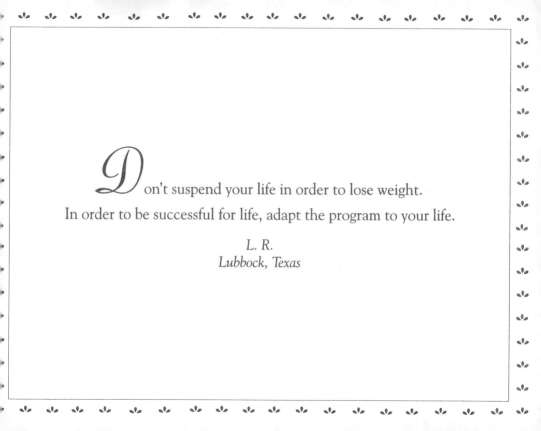

$\mathcal{D}$on't suspend your life in order to lose weight.
In order to be successful for life, adapt the program to your life.

L. R.
Lubbock, Texas

*M*easure everything. Portion sizes are sometimes
smaller than we think they are, but the food plan
has so many choices that you'll never feel deprived.

S. G.
Portland, North Dakota

$\mathcal{K}$eep a diary, not just of what you eat but also of your moods and feelings. You'll find clues to your progress— what people and places helped you stay in control.

C. S.
Stamford, Connecticut